The India Paintings

For YOU

I have been a painter all my life. My work has always been an expression of my heart and my intention has been to paint the beauty of the world we live in.

The aim of my work is to convey an experience of timelessness through color. Colors, in connection with forms, such as landscapes, can have transforming effects on people. There is an extraordinary energy in color – a deep interconnection with life itself. I am intrigued by the potential for healing energy to flow from my art.

Inspired by my frequent trips to India, my spiritual practice has given me insight into two key ingredients of creativity: being present in the moment so that creativity may flow freely, and the cultivation of quietude which allows our "inner voice" to speak its unique artistic language, unhindered by outer distractions. With practice, the creative flow becomes as natural as breathing – and art becomes the expression of an unfolding awareness of that which exists both within and without.

While traveling, I snap photographs of my environment and paint in watercolors. Upon returning home, these smaller works and images are transformed into oil paintings. I also paint in Plein Air with oils and watercolors. I am inspired by landscapes, as the sky and the ways to represent it are endless. Color, shadows, and light play with design, and I enjoy the creation of color blends and forms.

My paintings have been displayed in galleries across the country, including numerous shows in New York City, and my work is owned in private collections around the world. Several of my paintings were acquired by the Harmony Pavilion Medical Arts Building in Atlantic City, New Jersey for their healing qualities.

I am the mother of three boys, and teach art to children, teenagers and adults in my home studio in Chatham, NJ. I am presently busy in my studio working on oil and watercolor paintings.

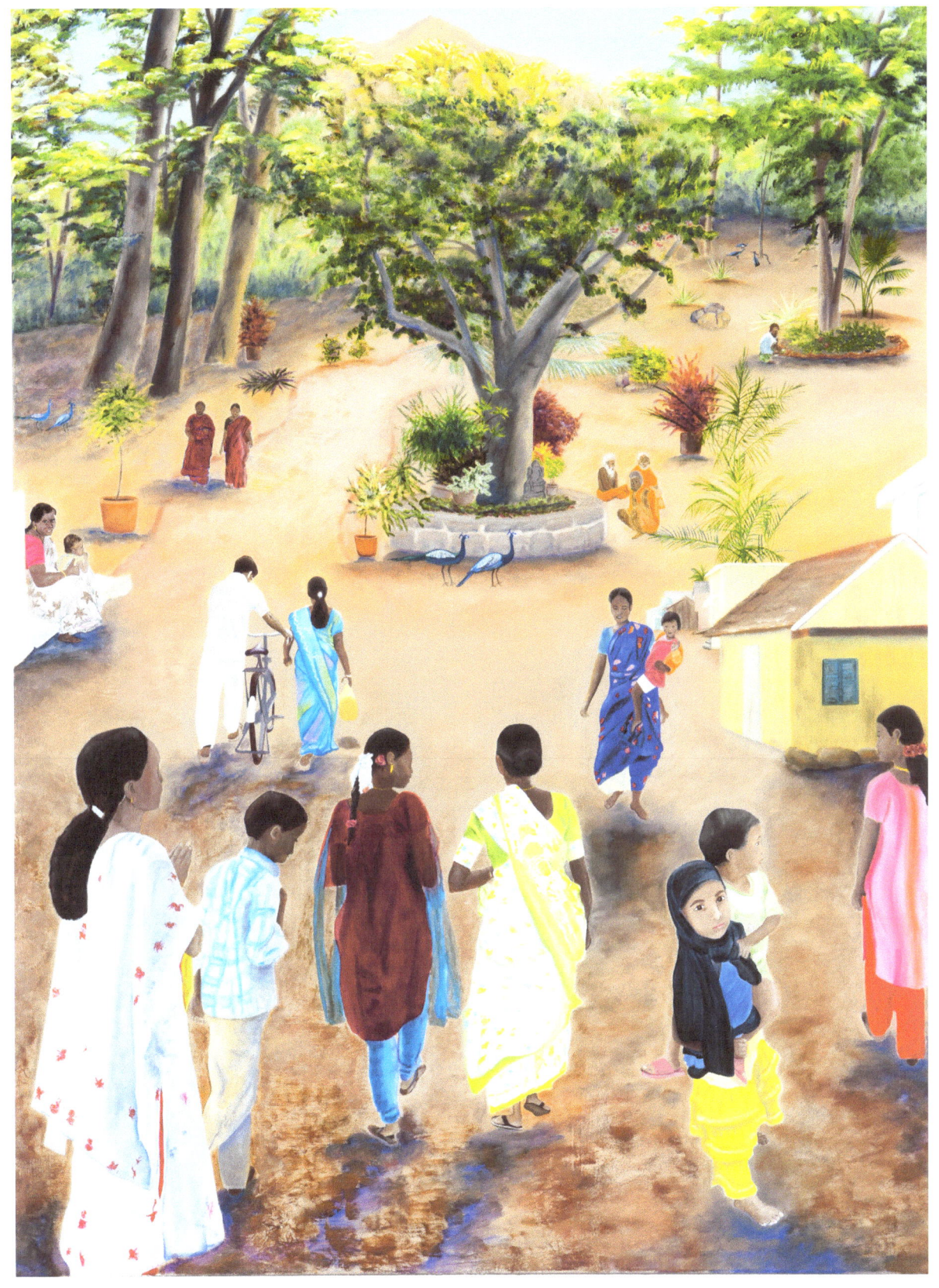

A Day in India

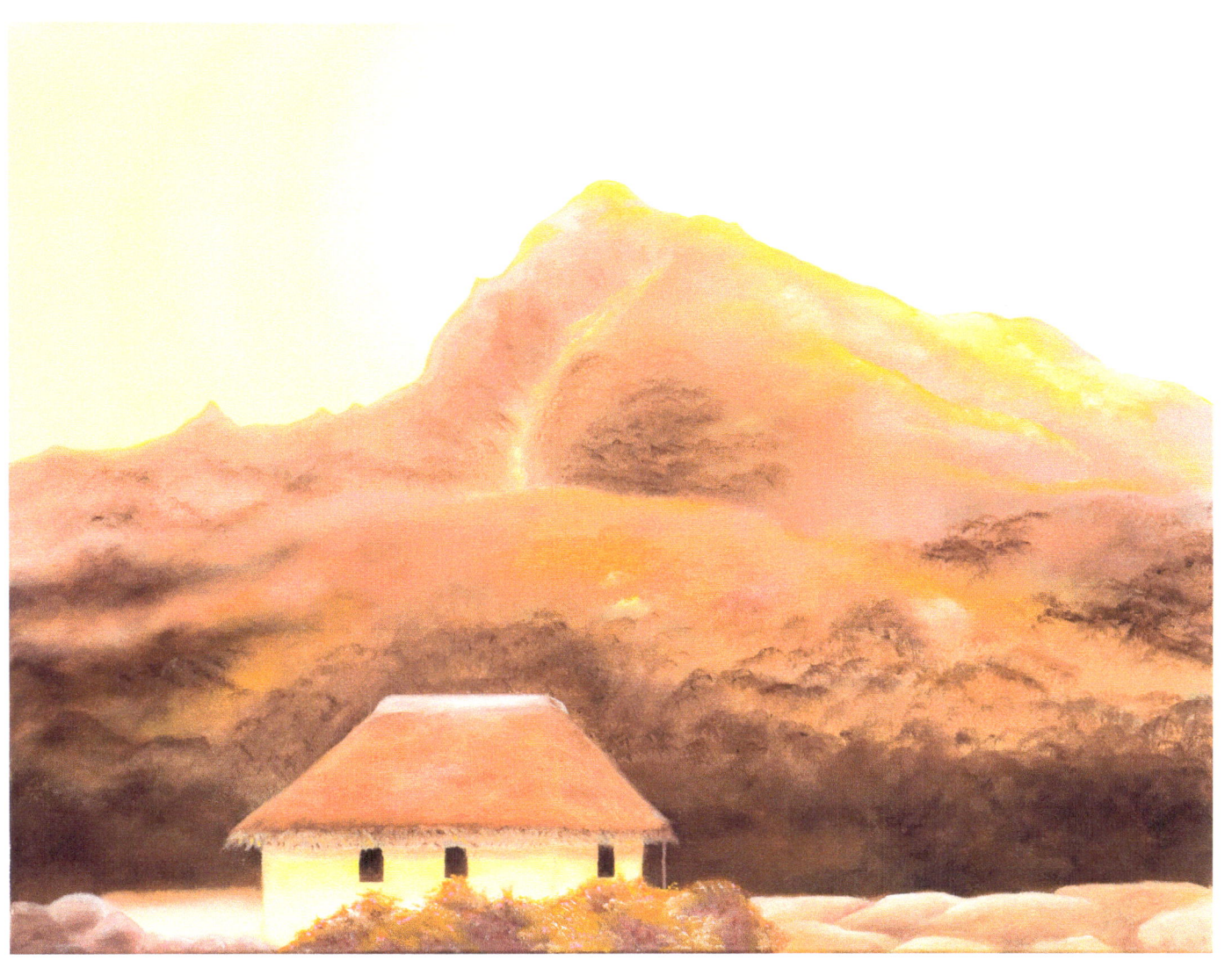

The Beginning

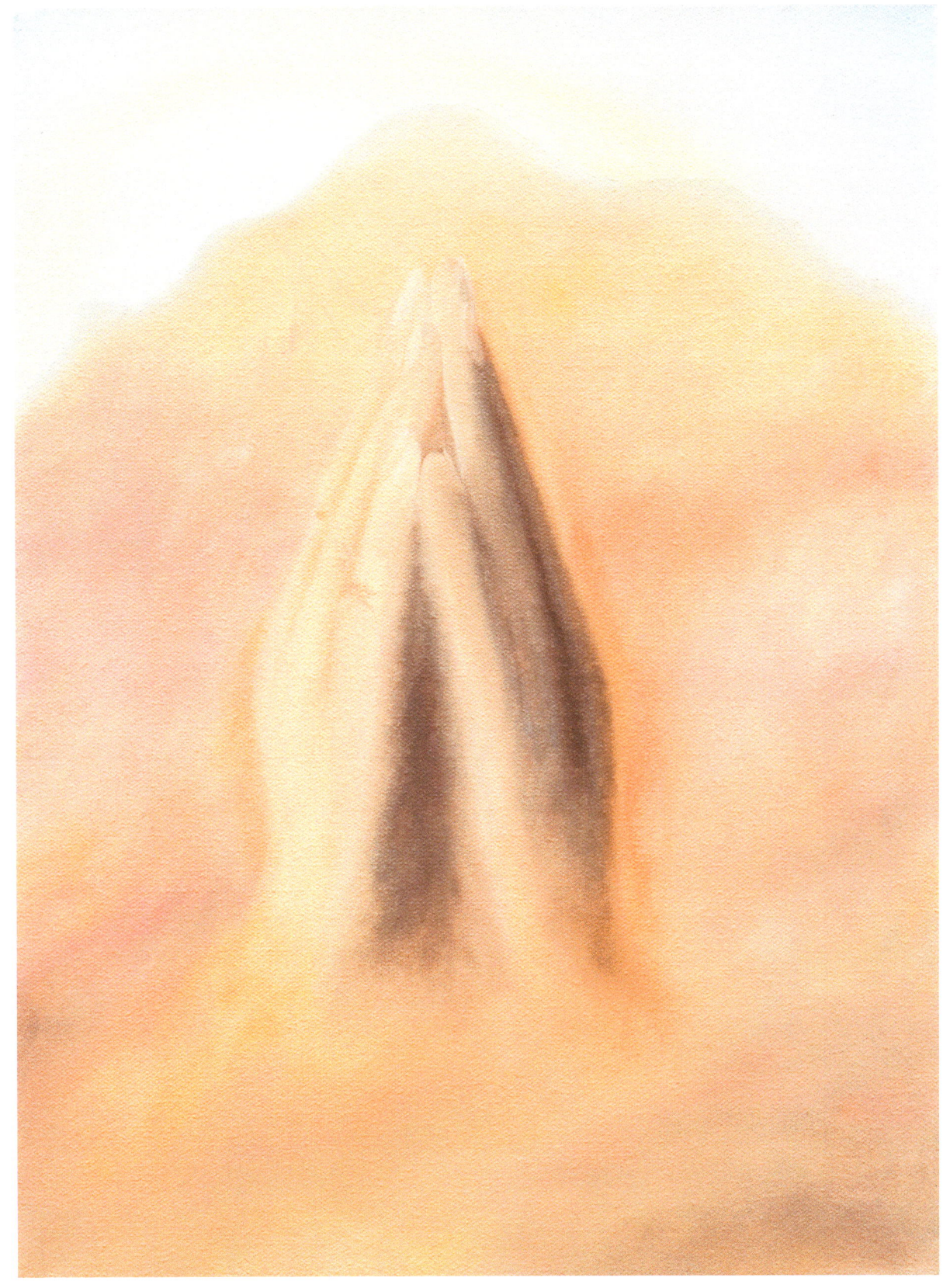

Namaste

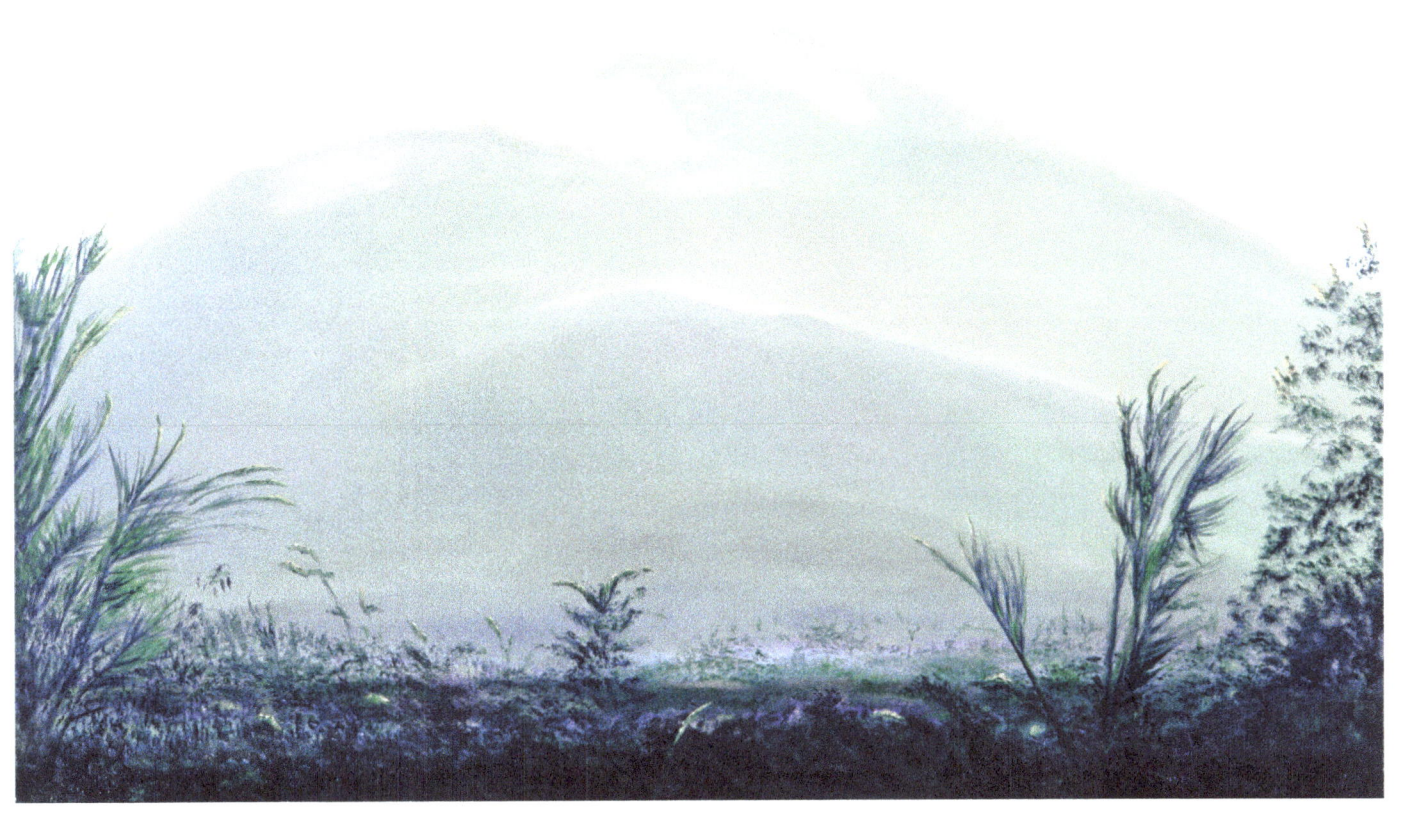

Mountain at Dawn

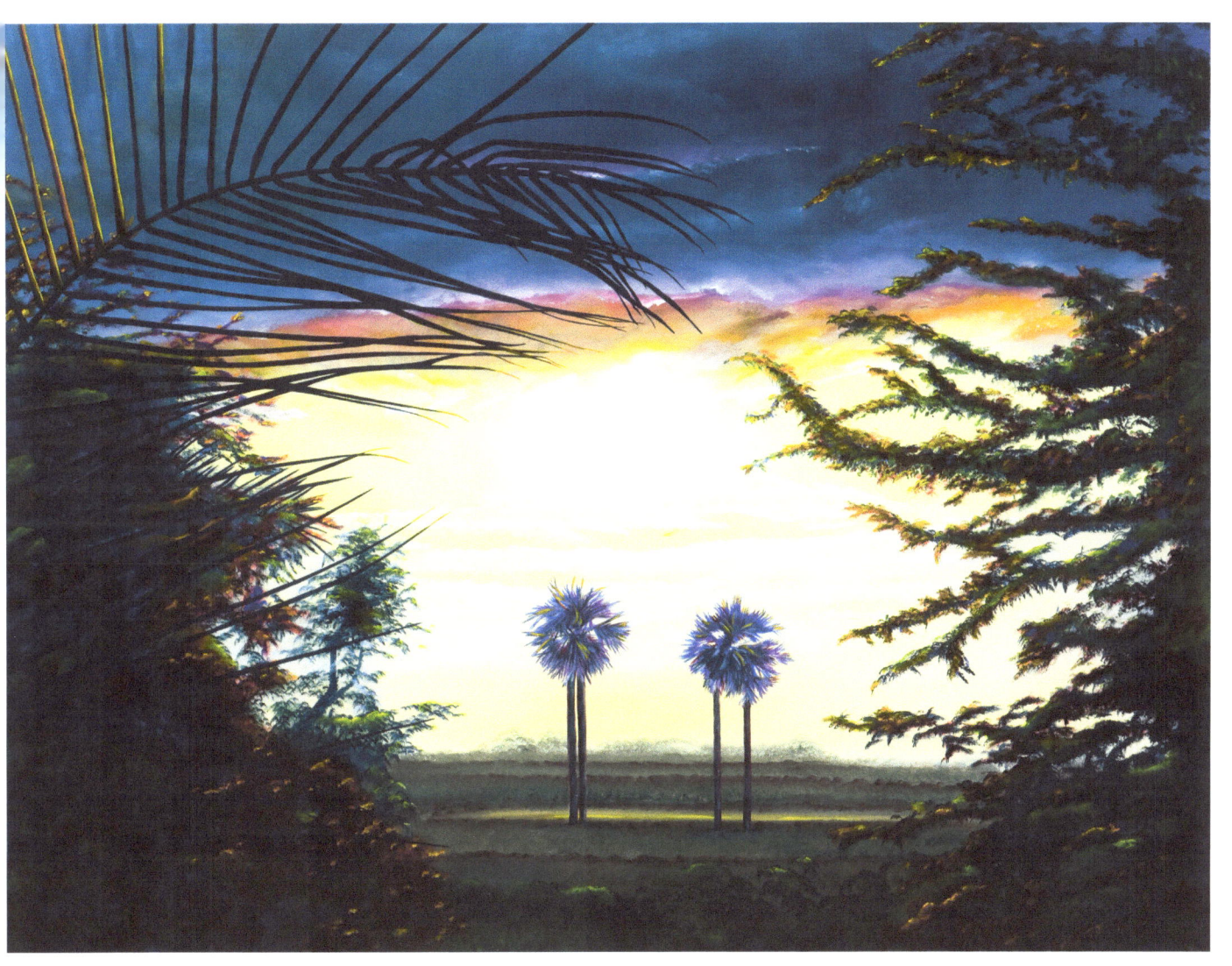

Darshan

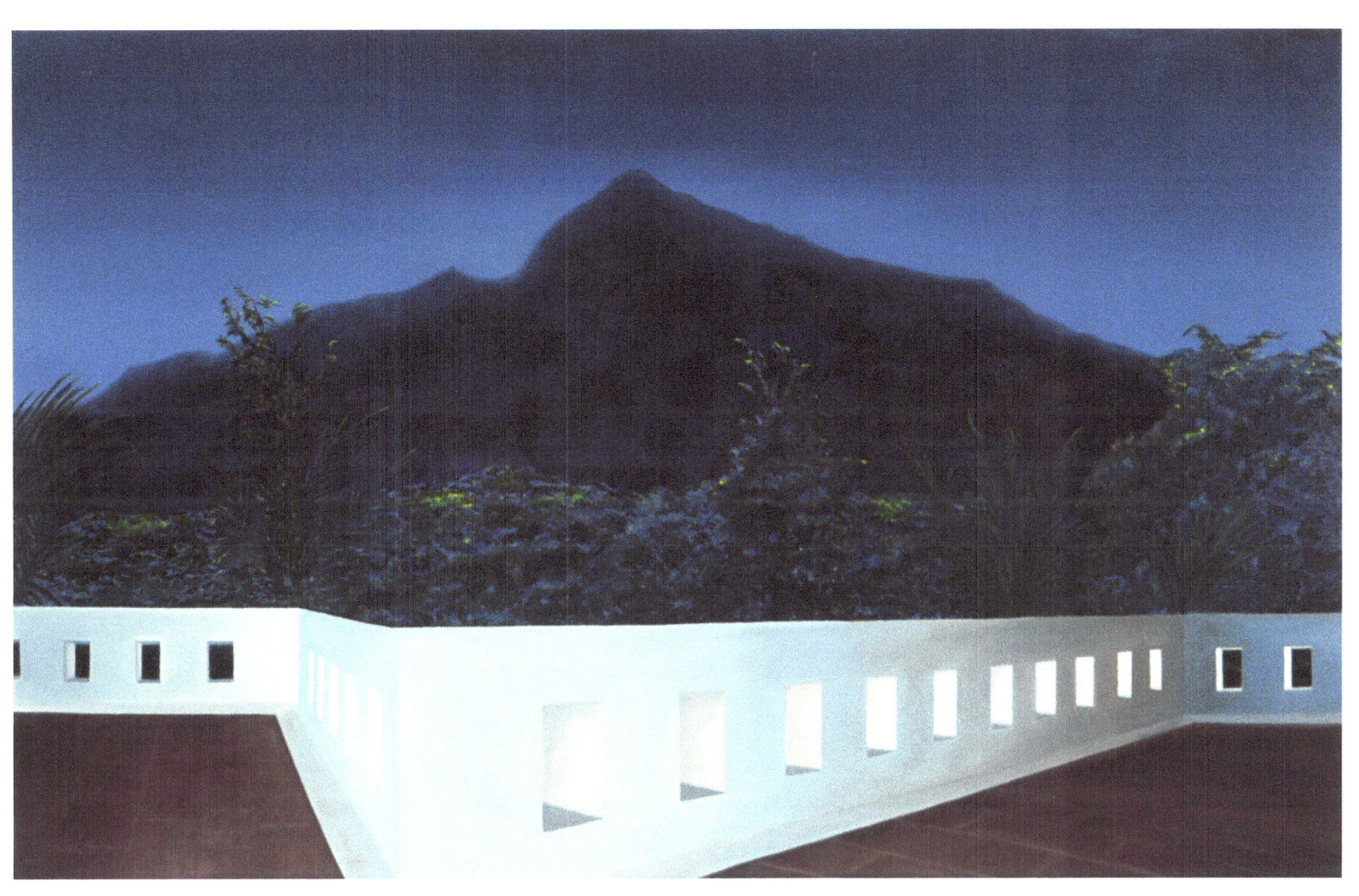

Beloved

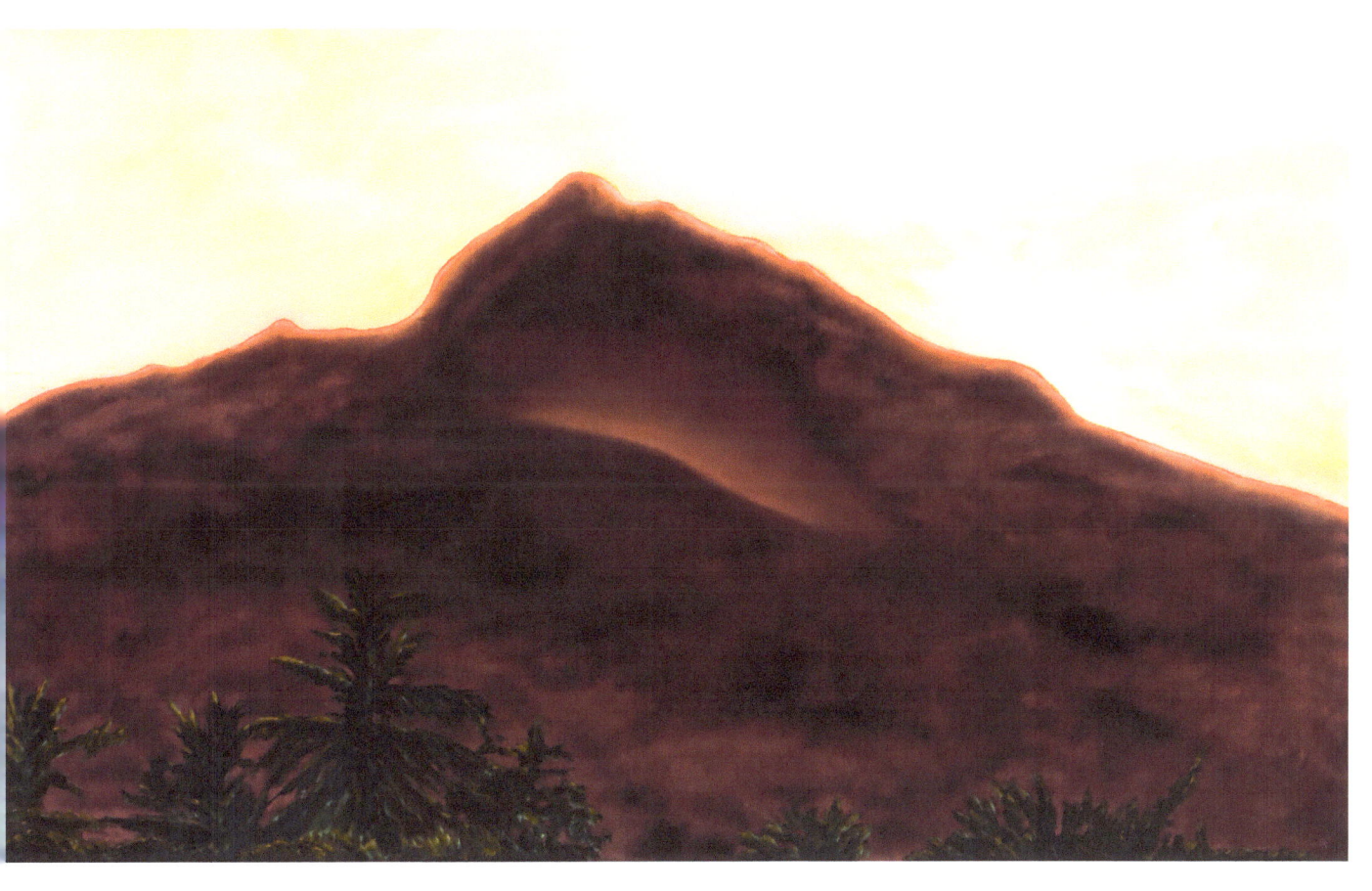

Aruna Mountain

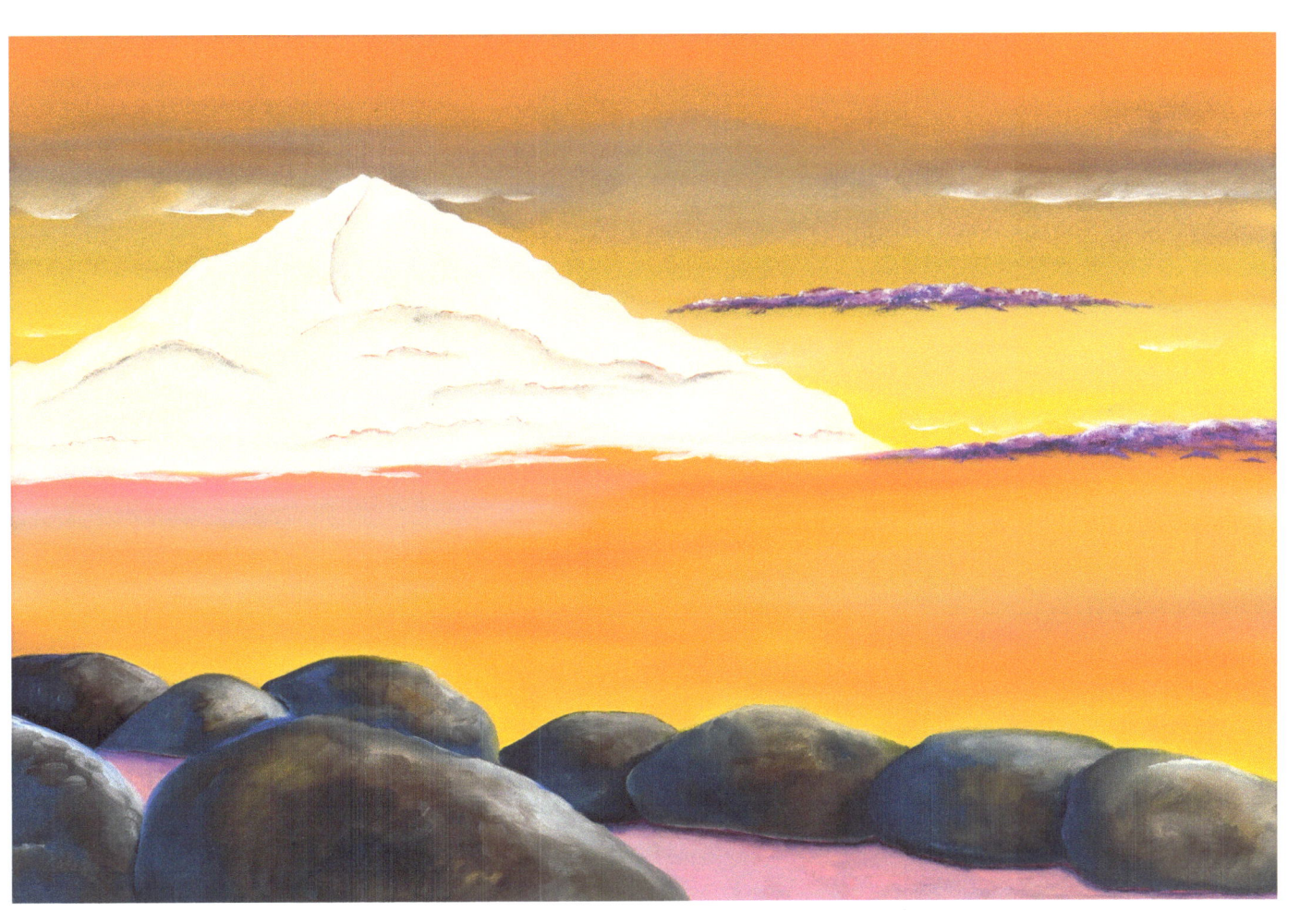

The Faraway Mountain

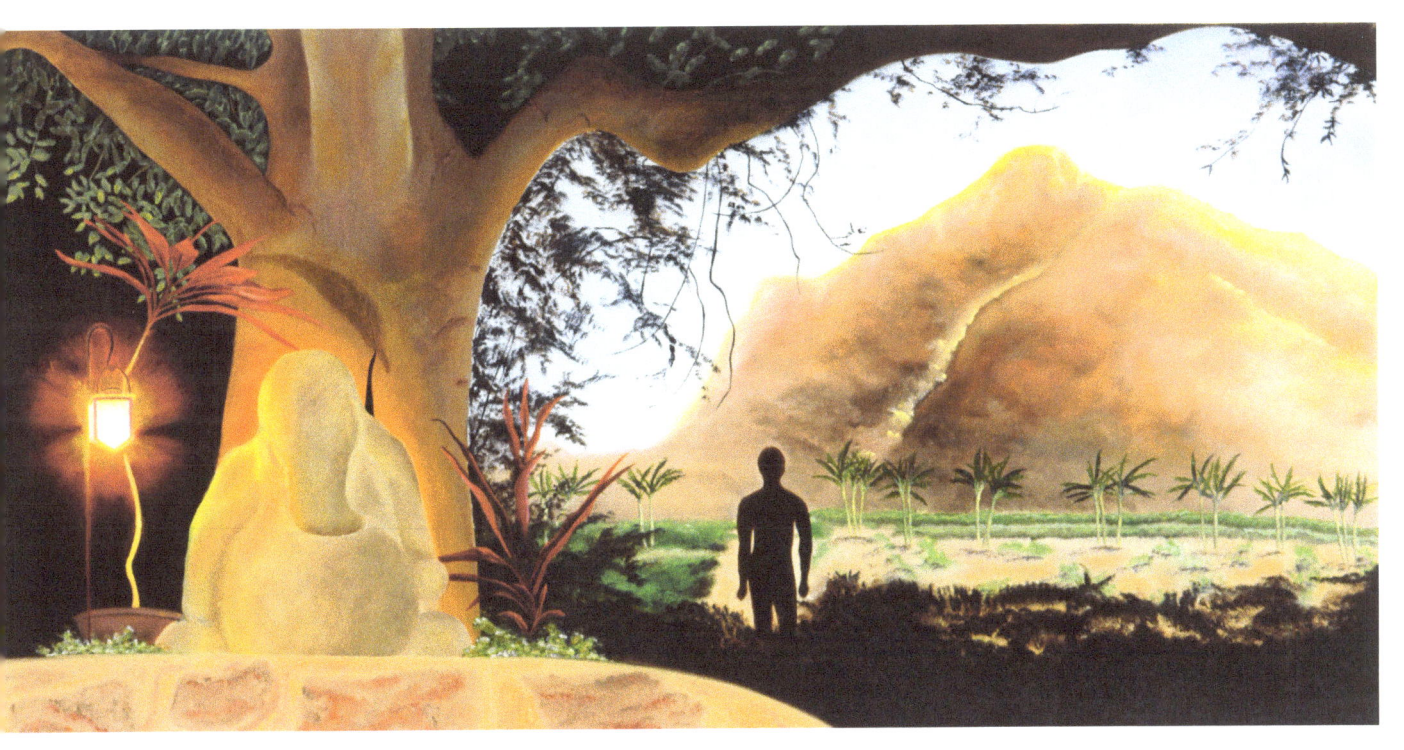

He Comes to Me

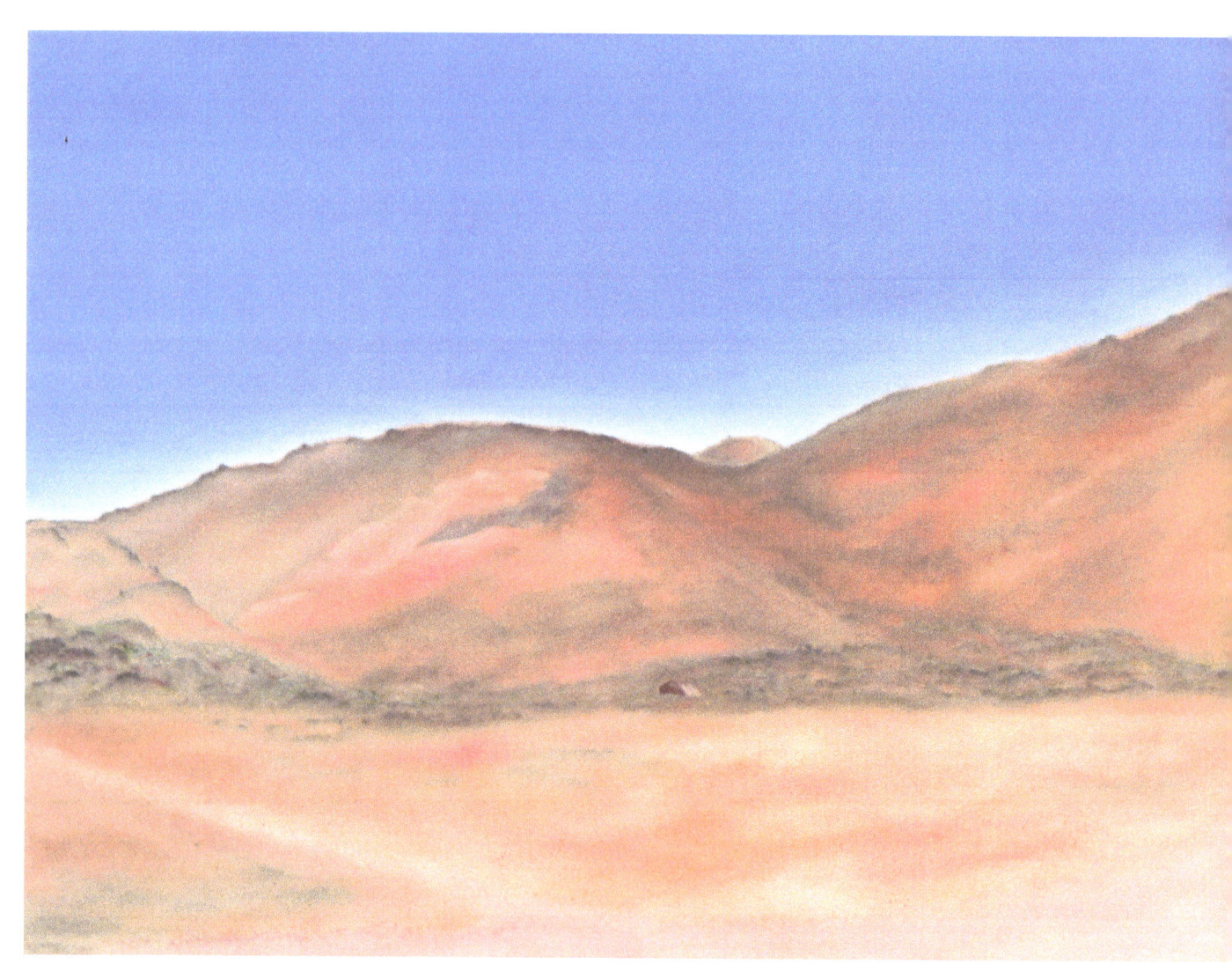

Surrender

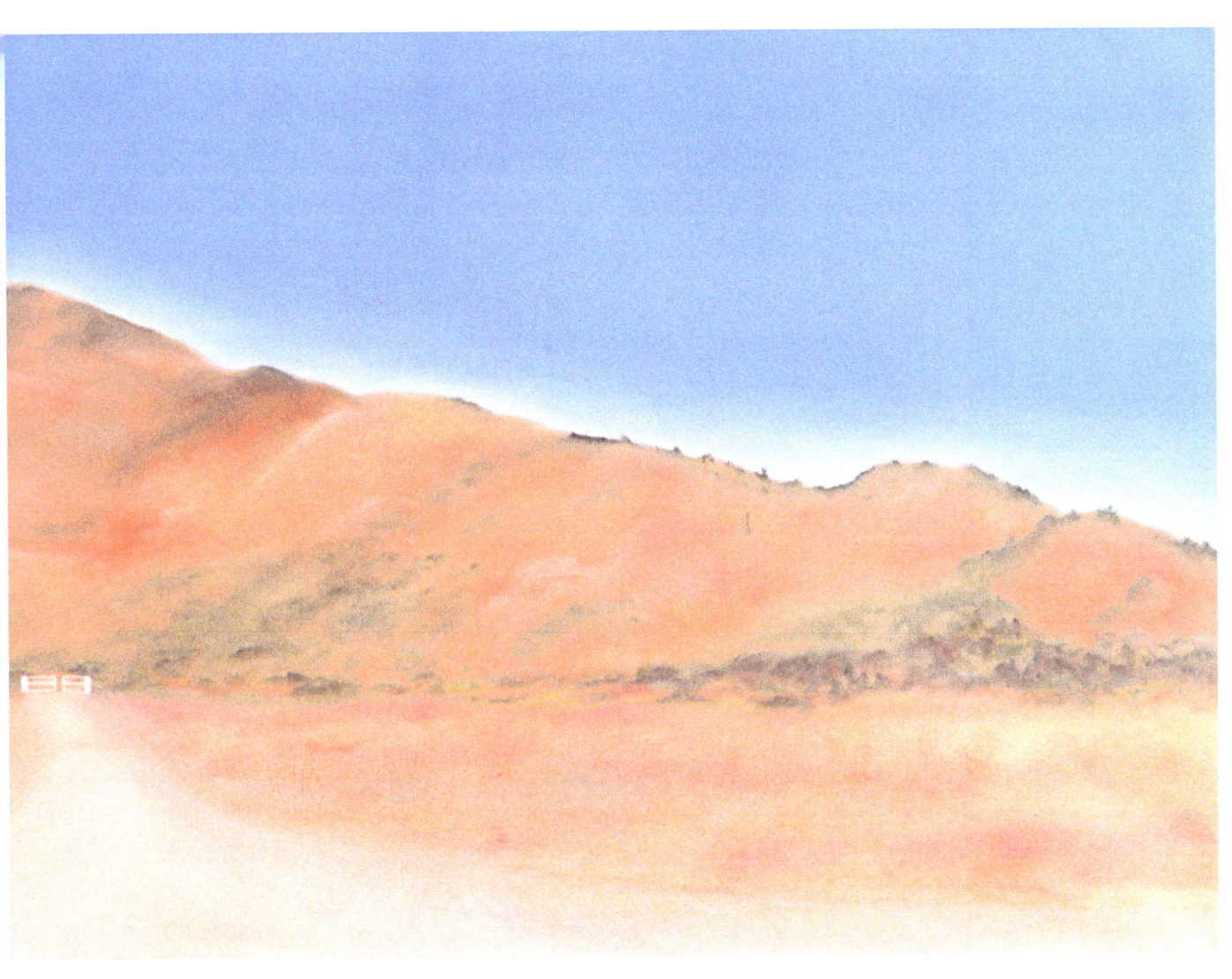

Mountain of Light

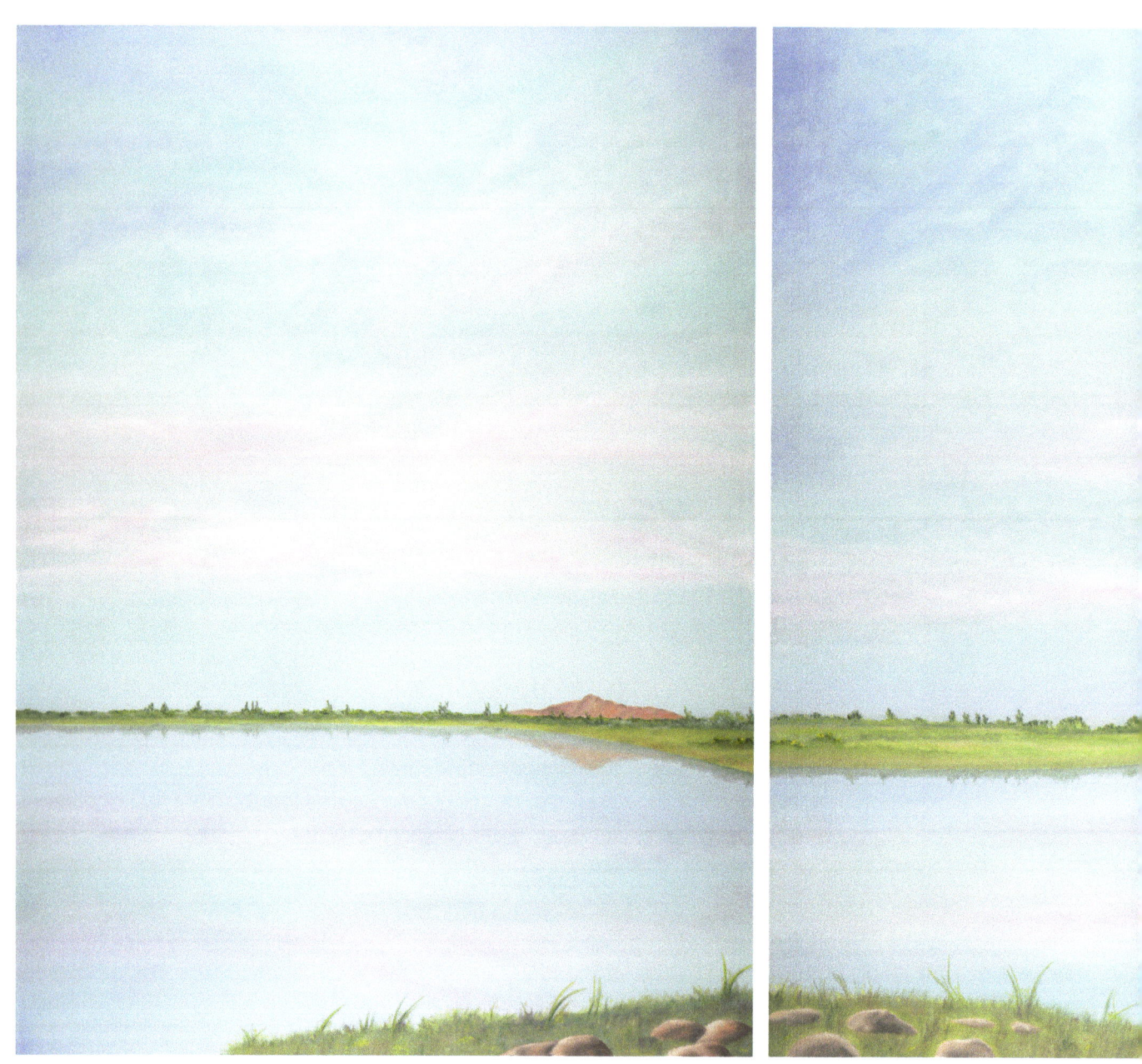

Deep Peace

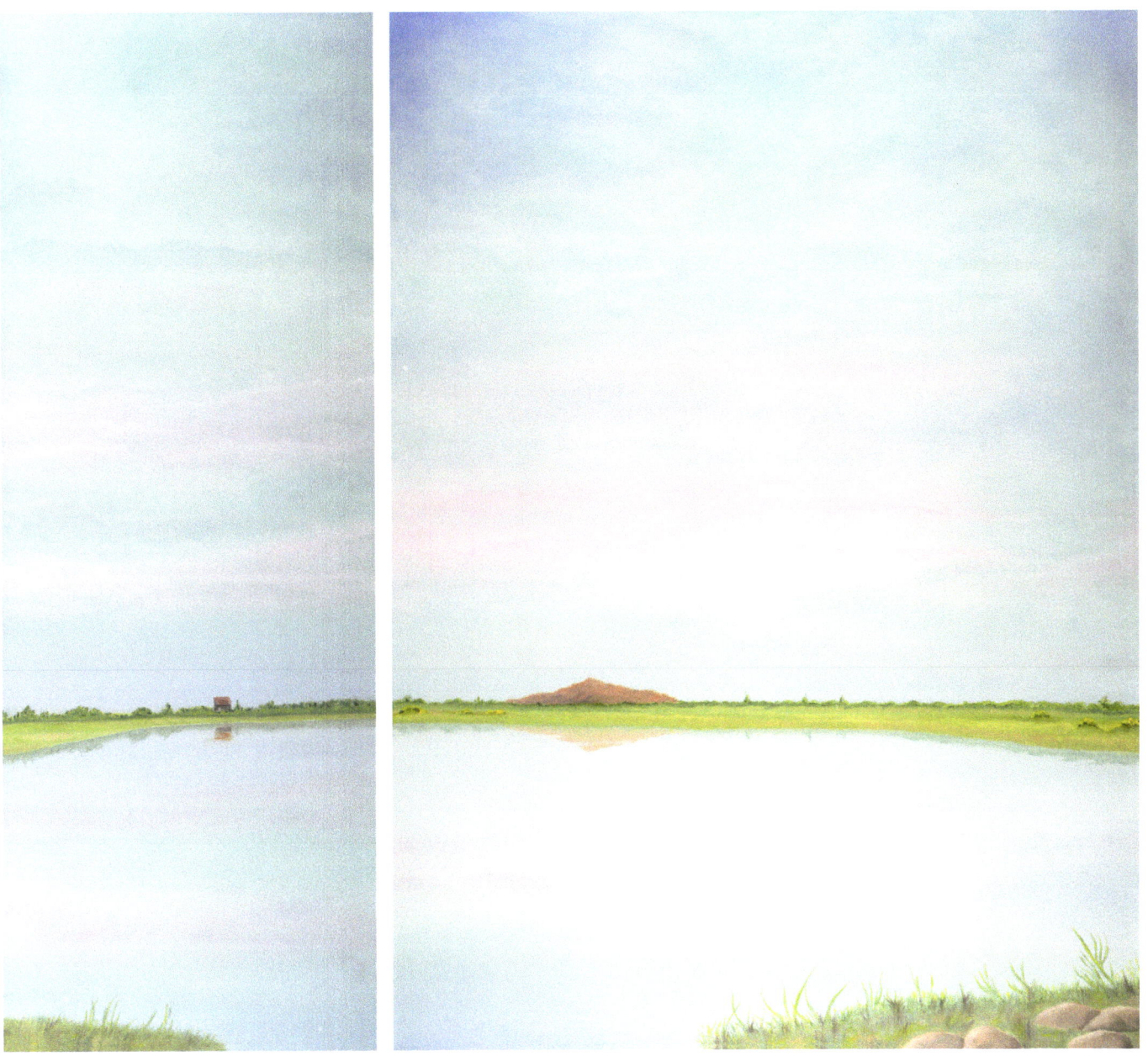

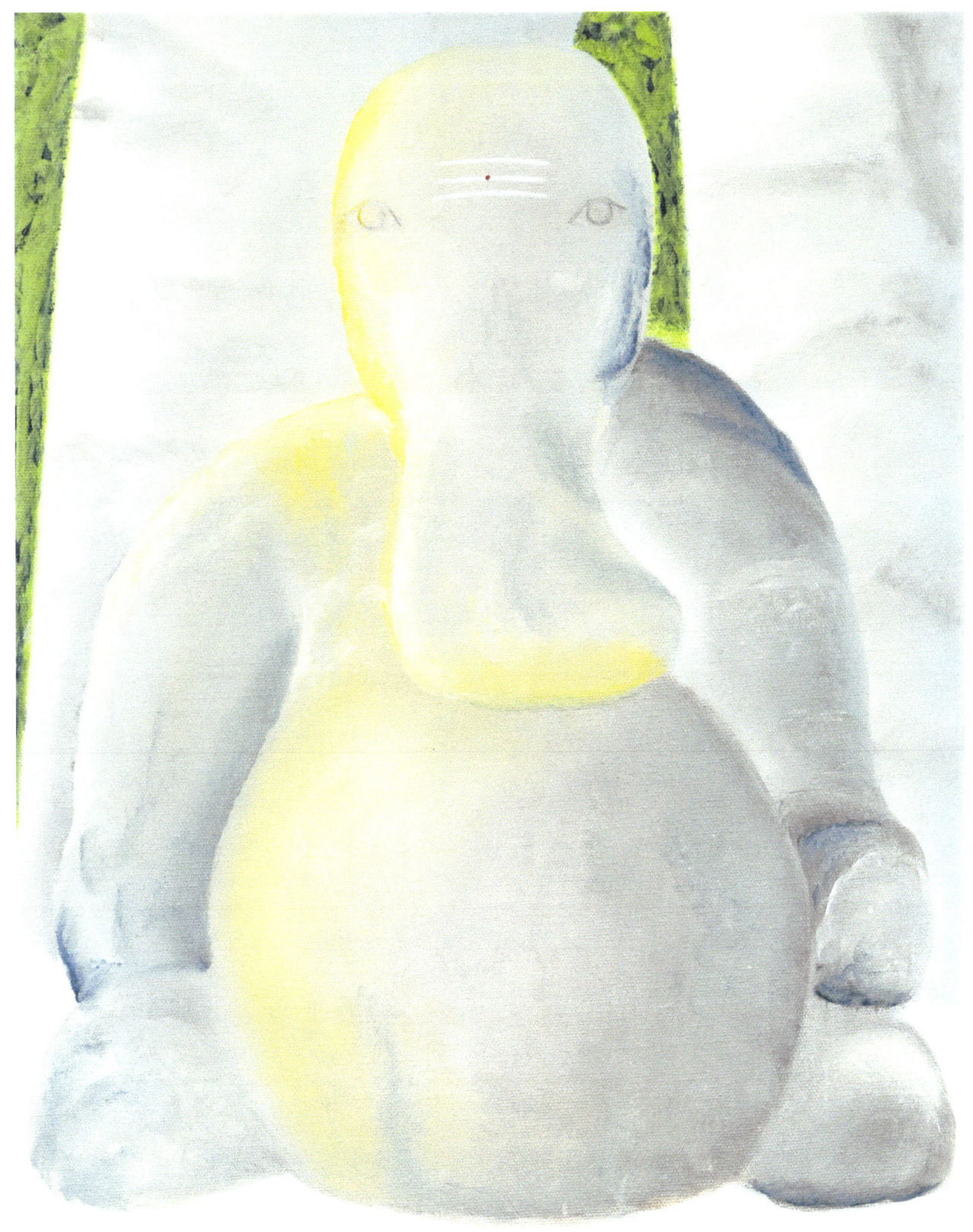

Ganesh II

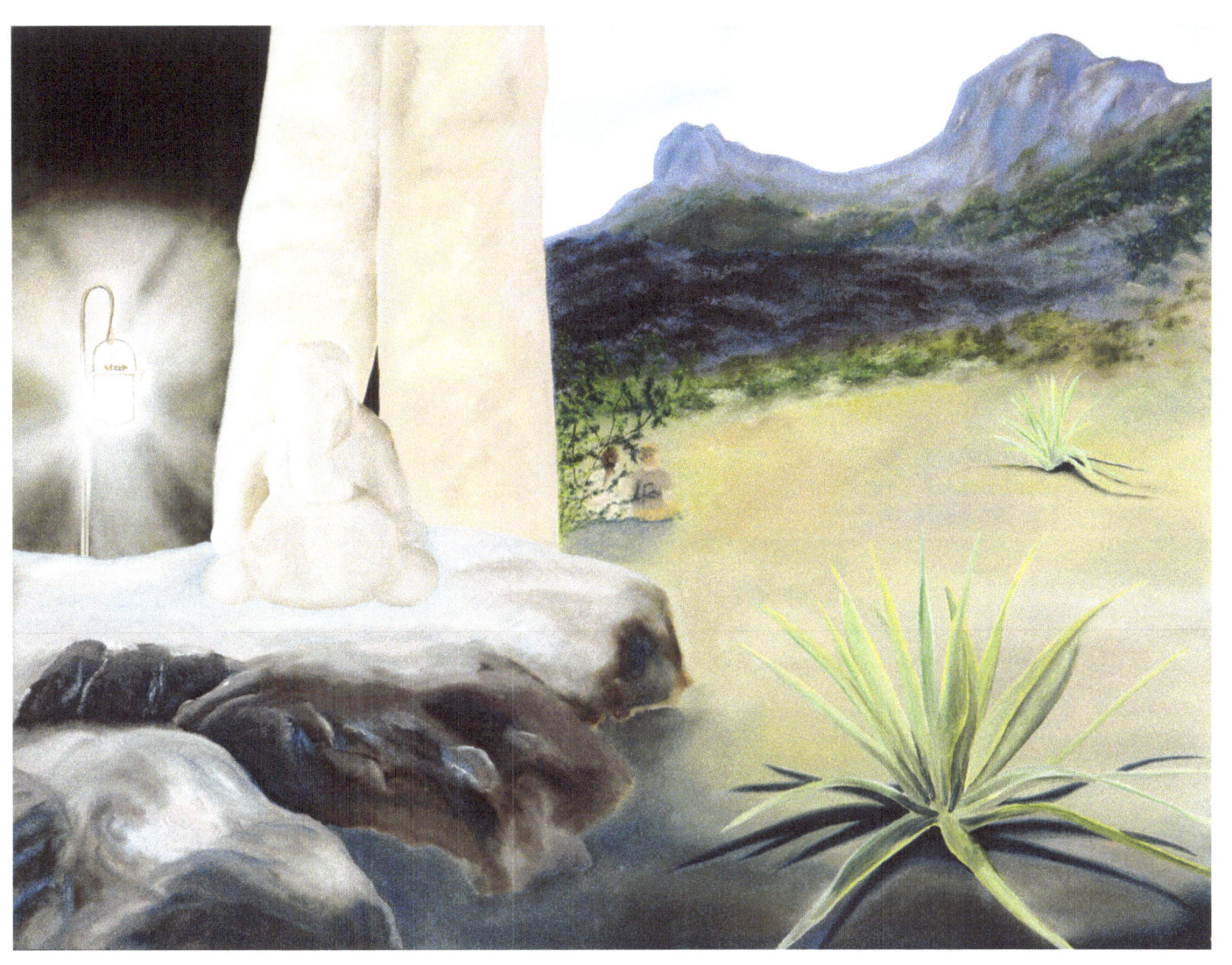

Untitled Peace

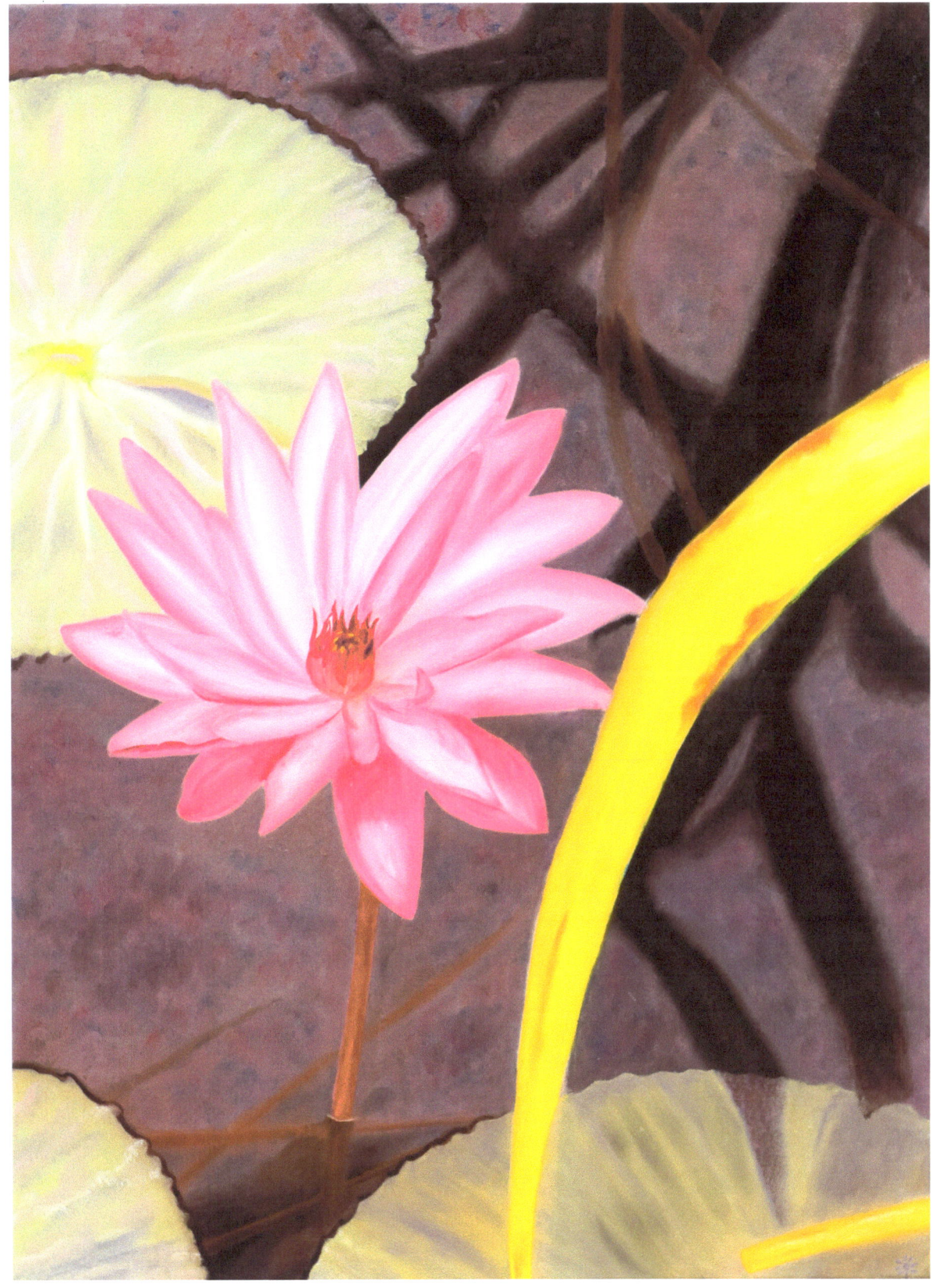

Lotus

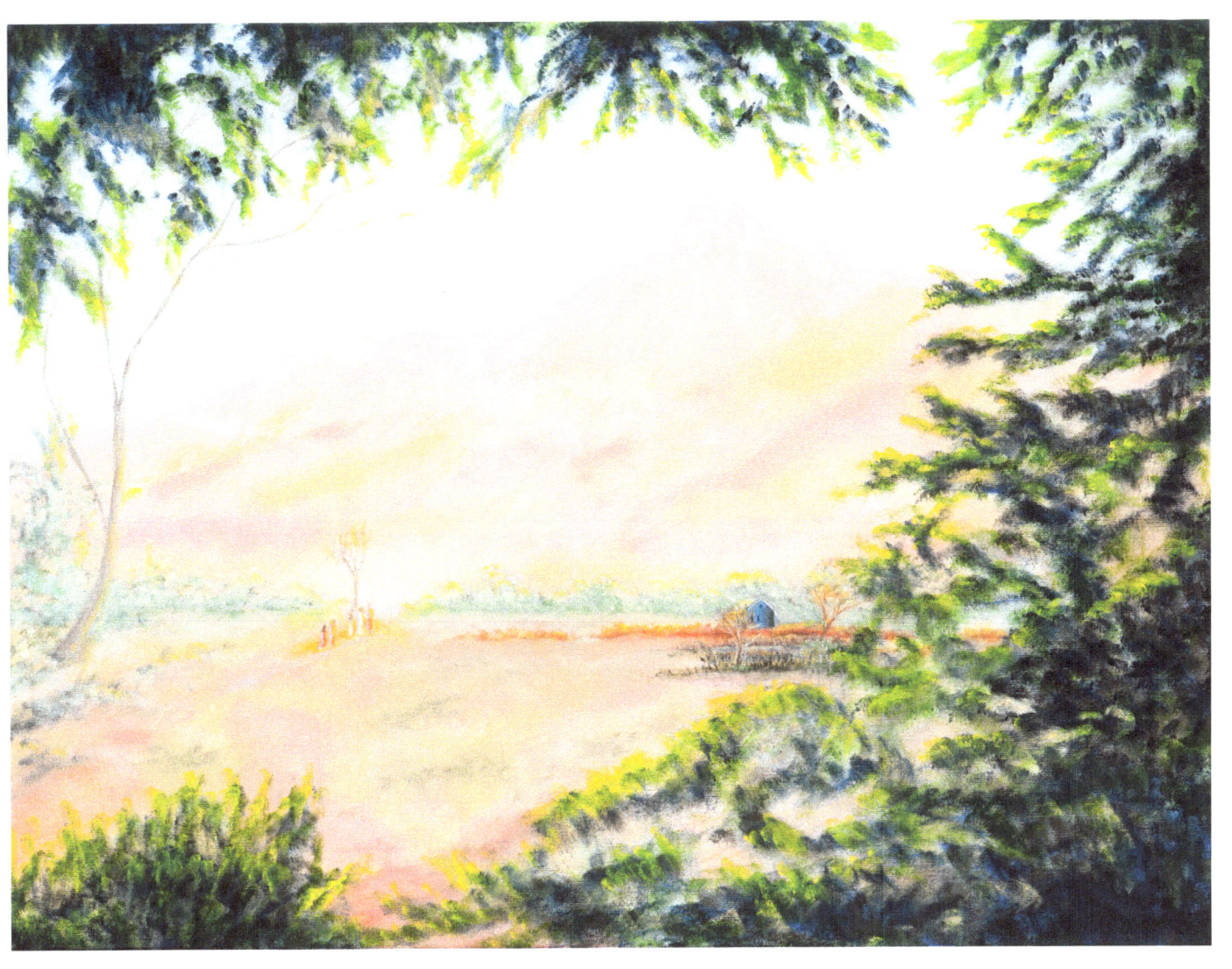

The Path

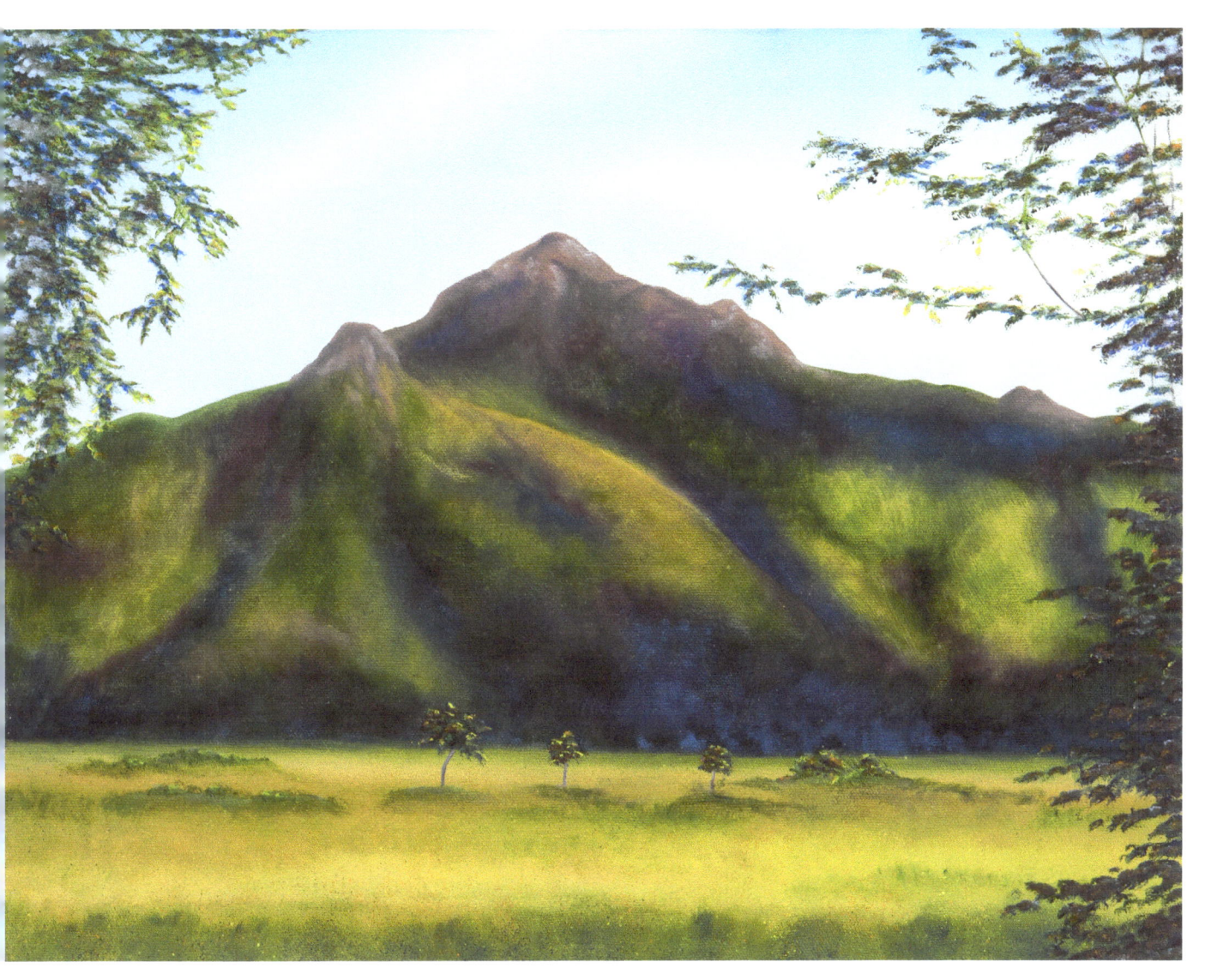

Green Mountain

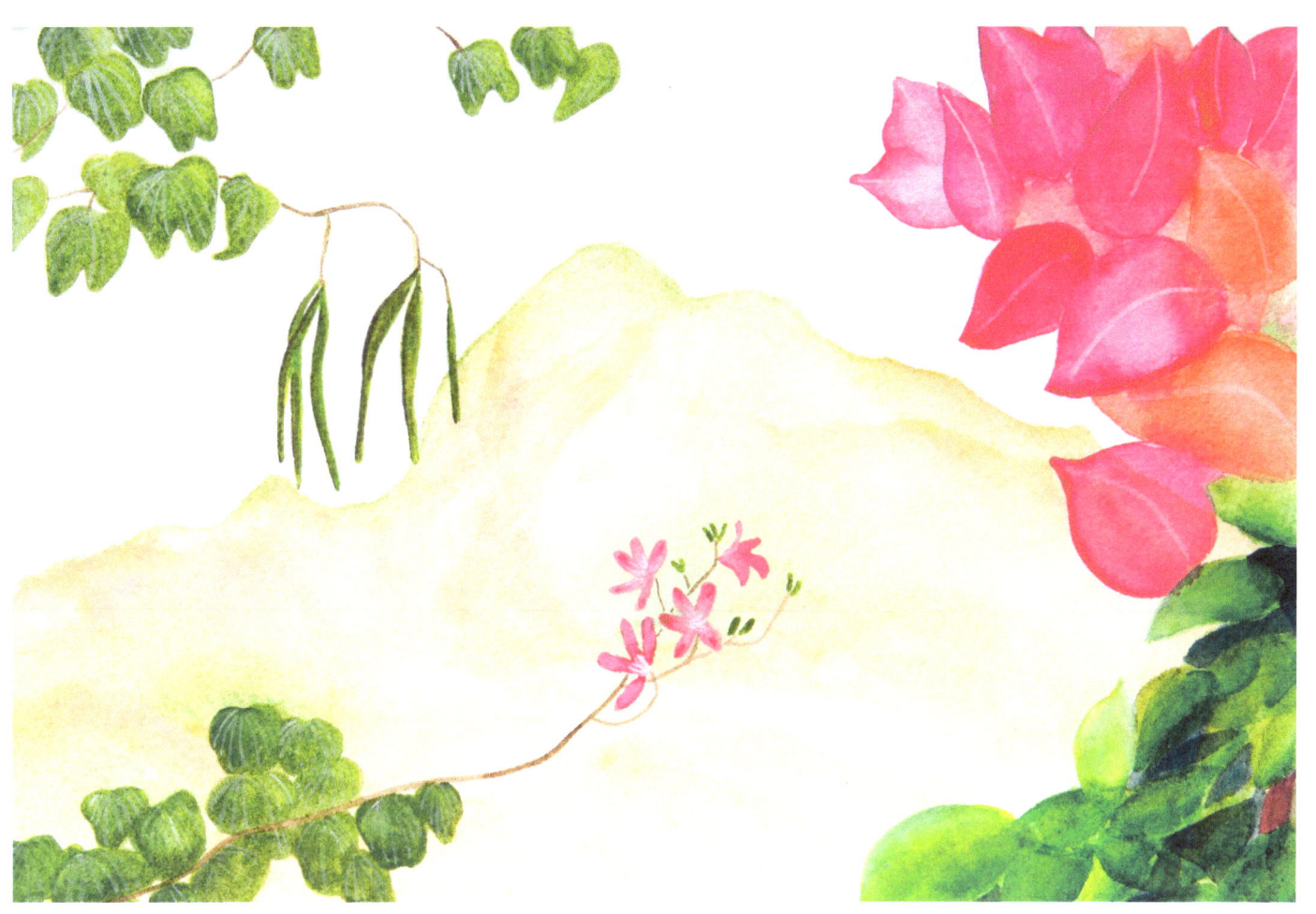

Flora II

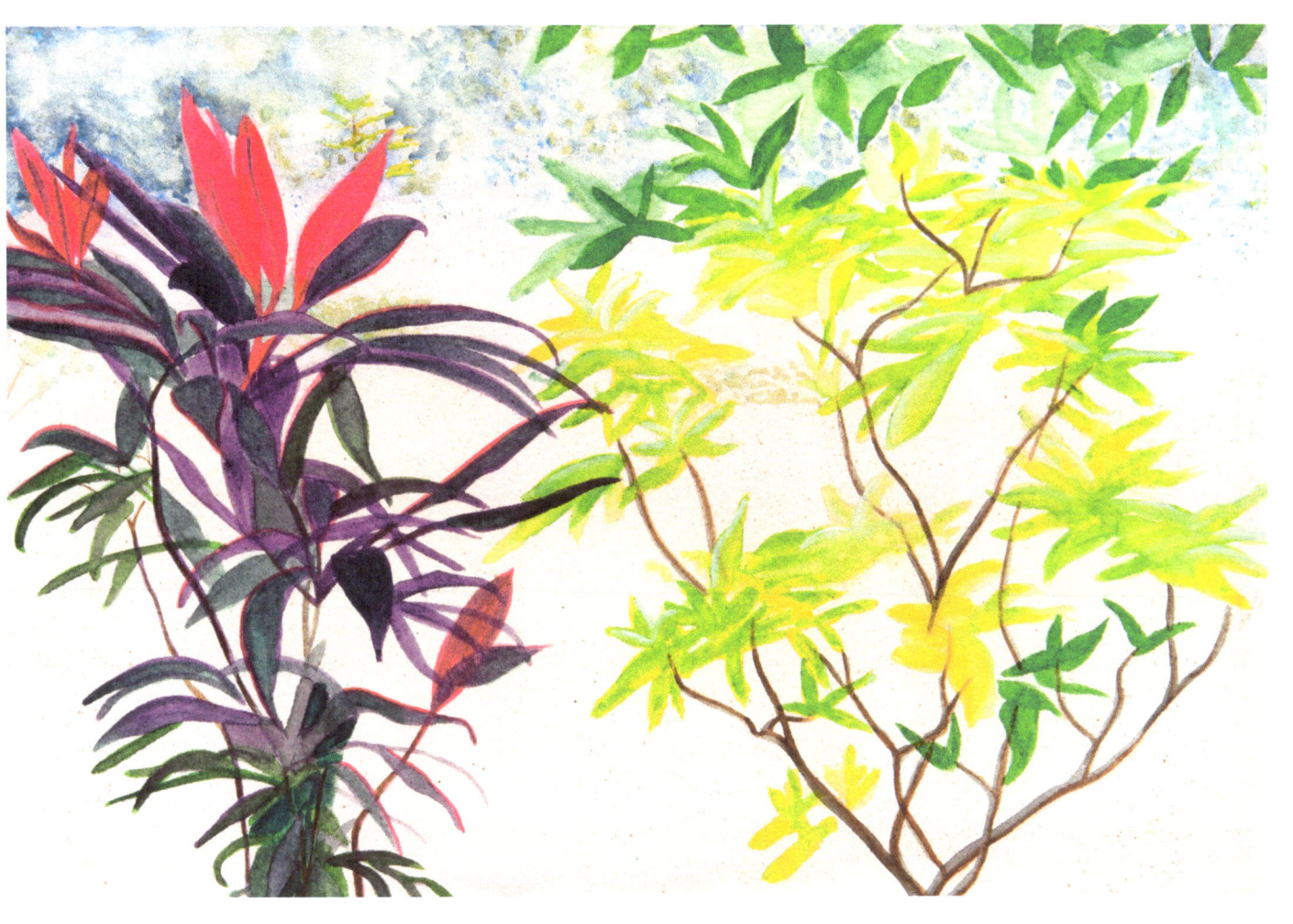

Flora III

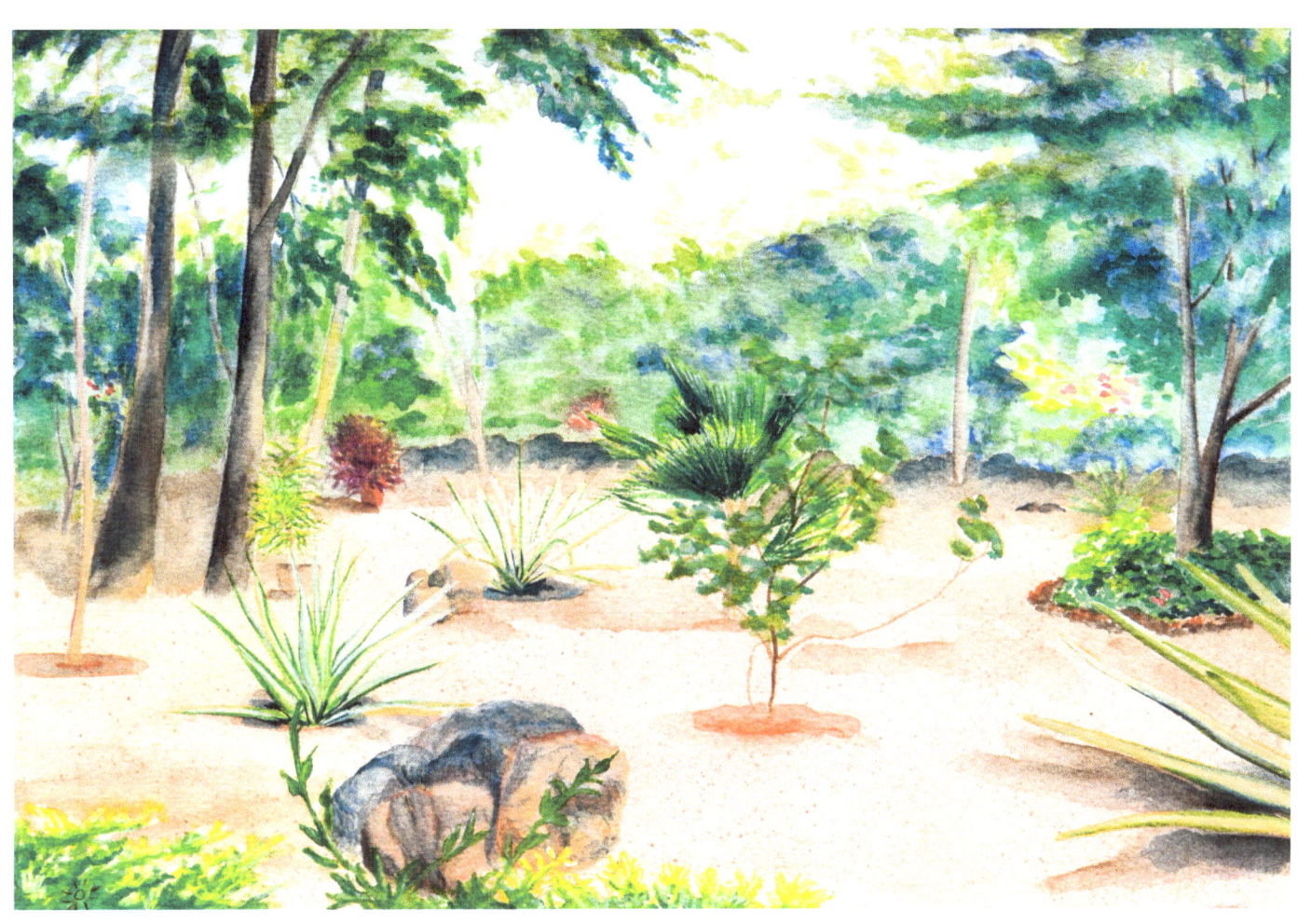

Flora IV

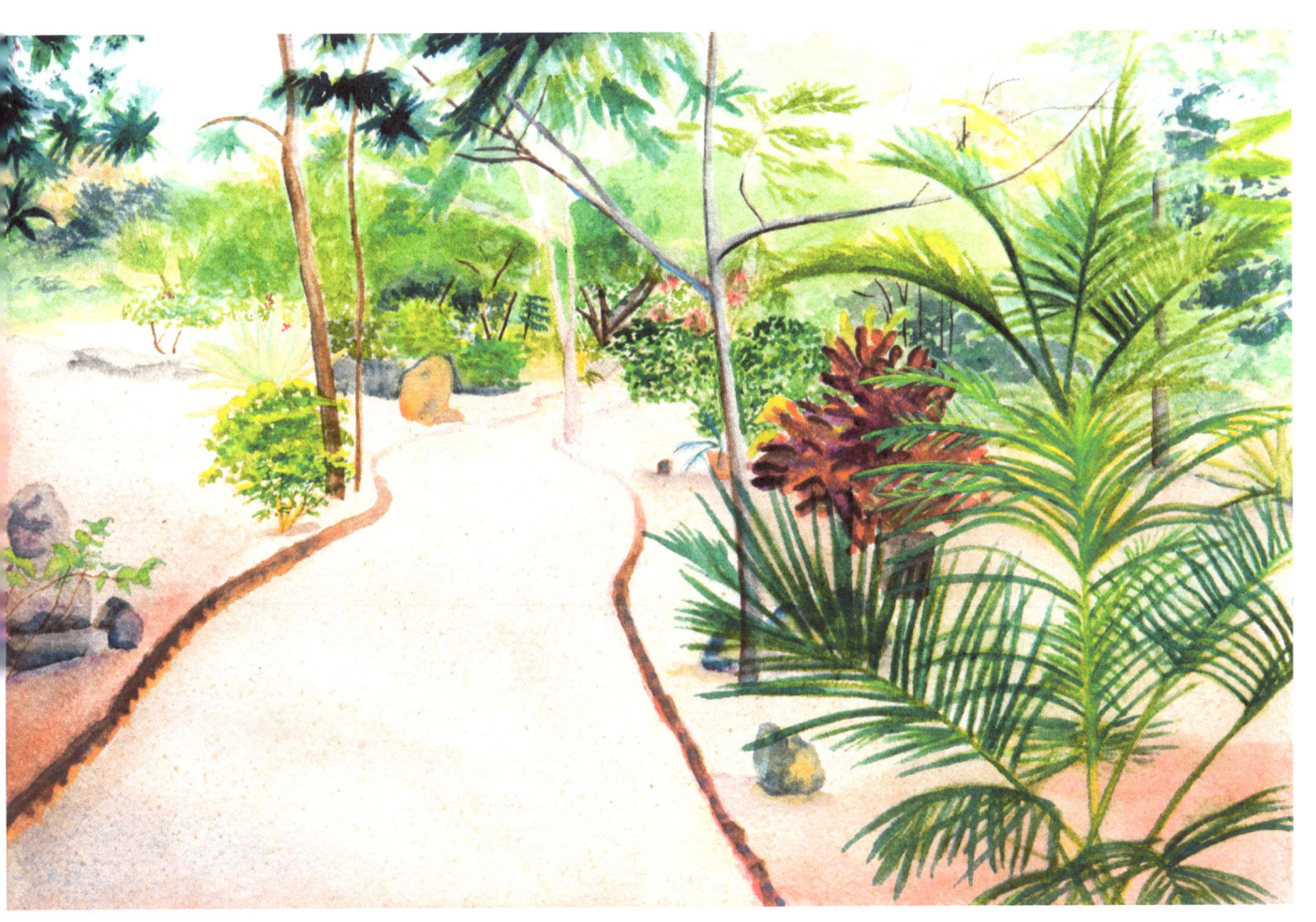

Flora V

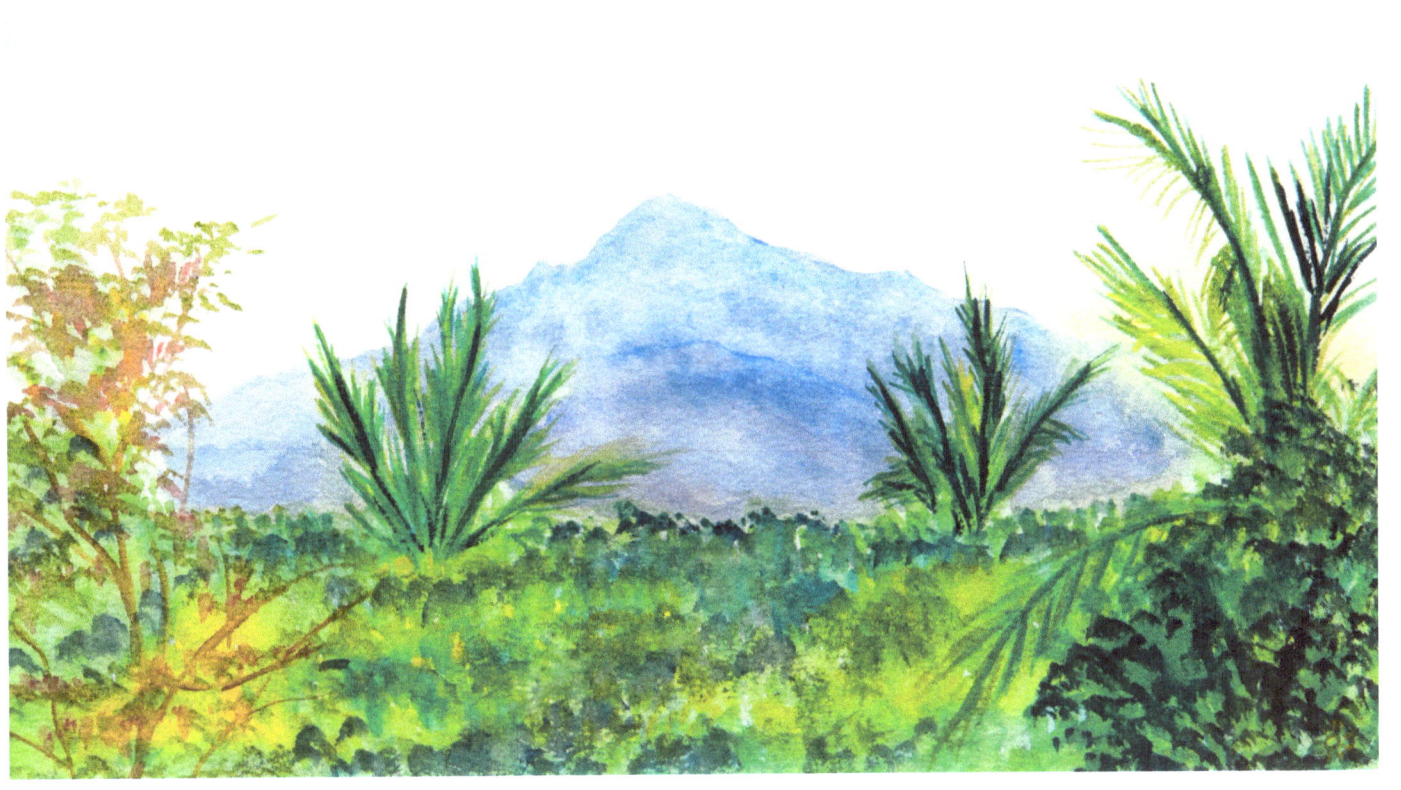

Flora I

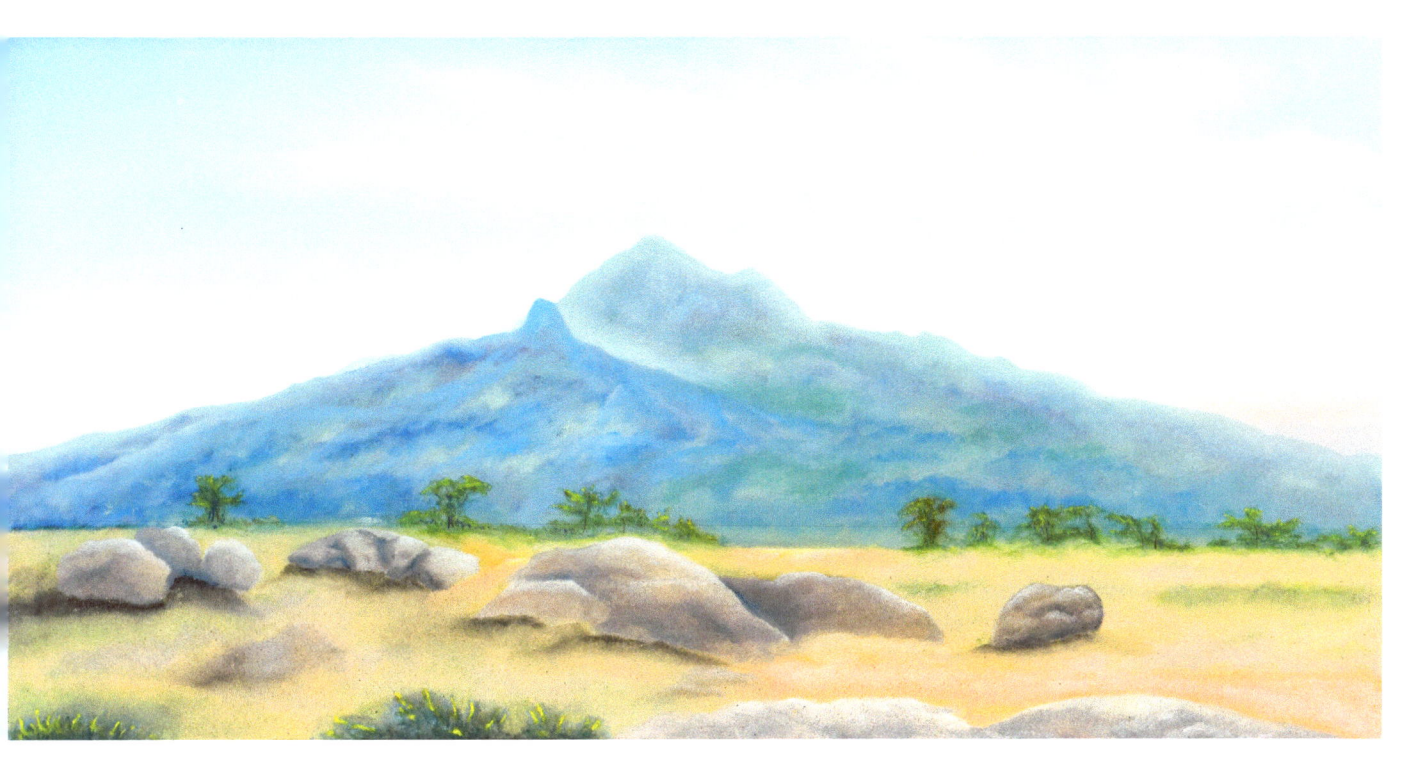

Behold the Mountain

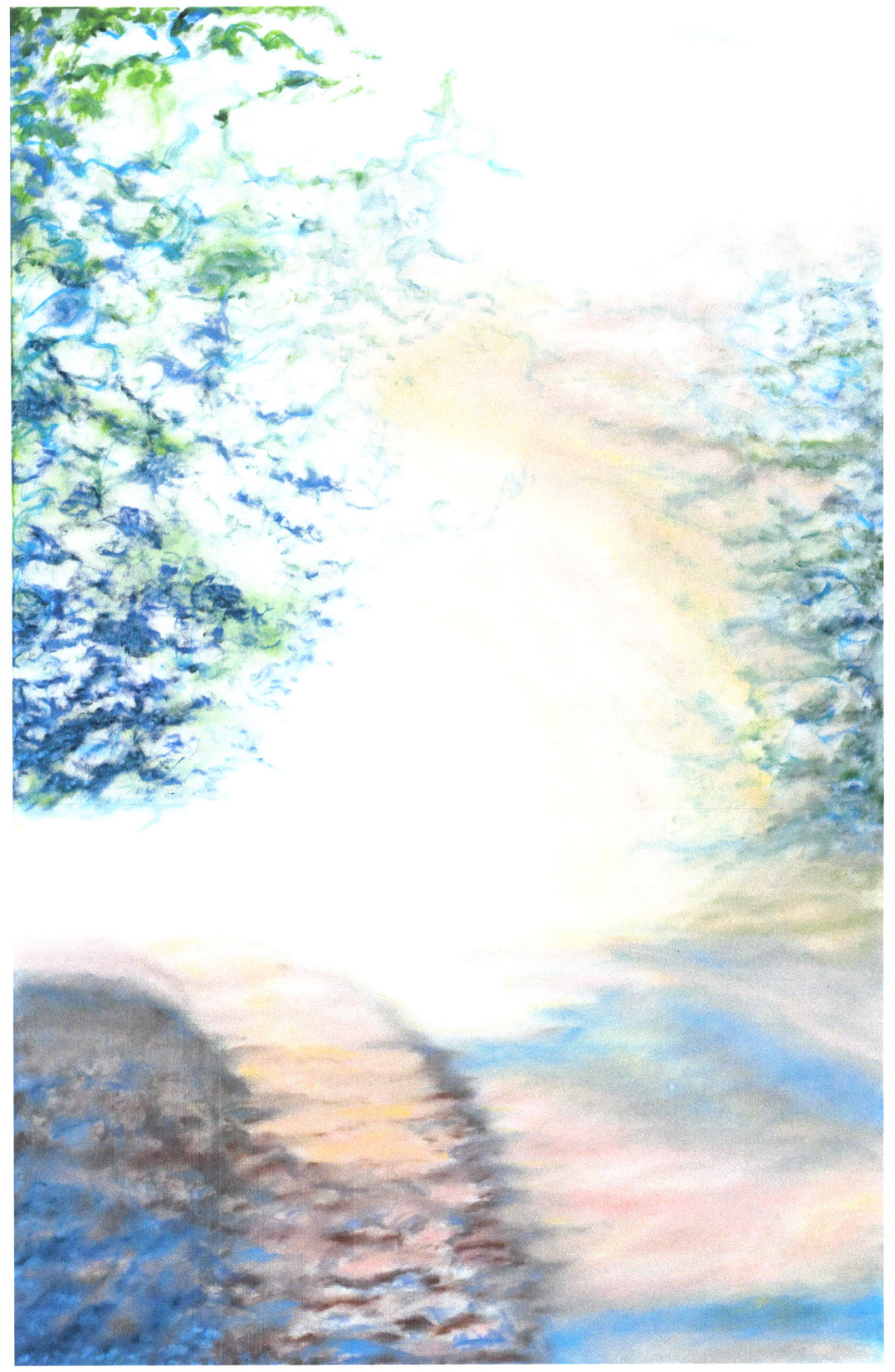

Pradakshina Path

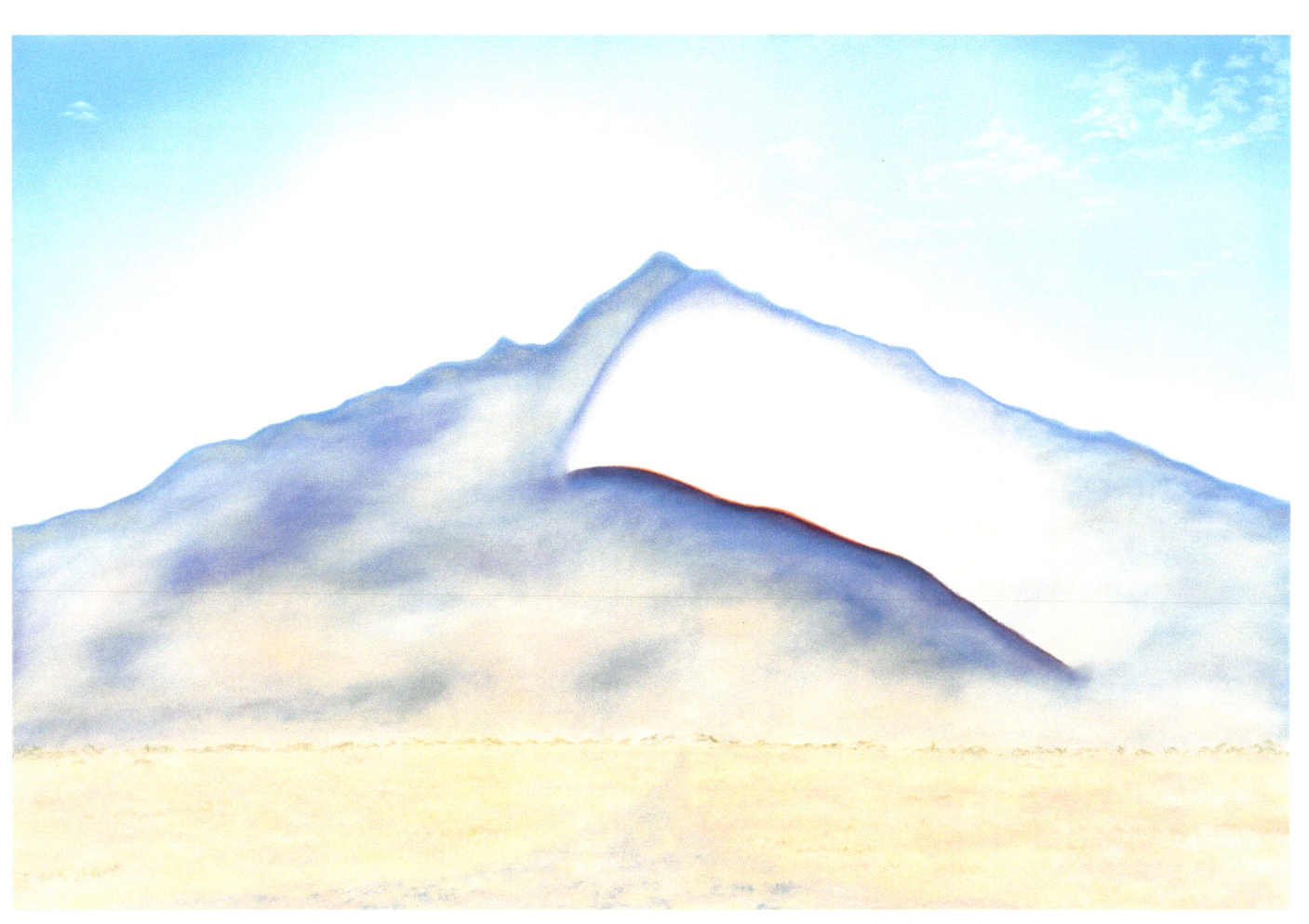

Home

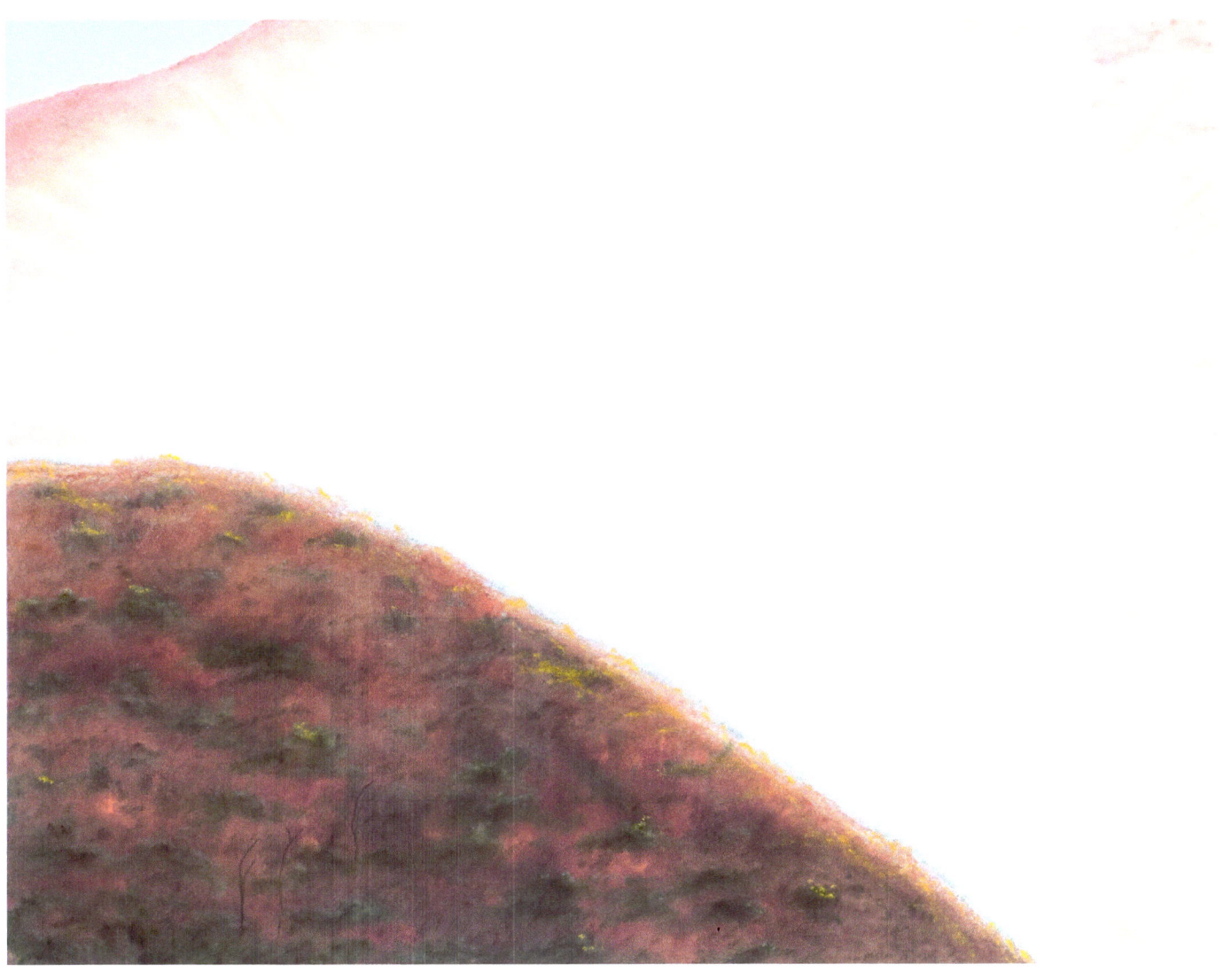

Home II

Home III

Home IV

Formless

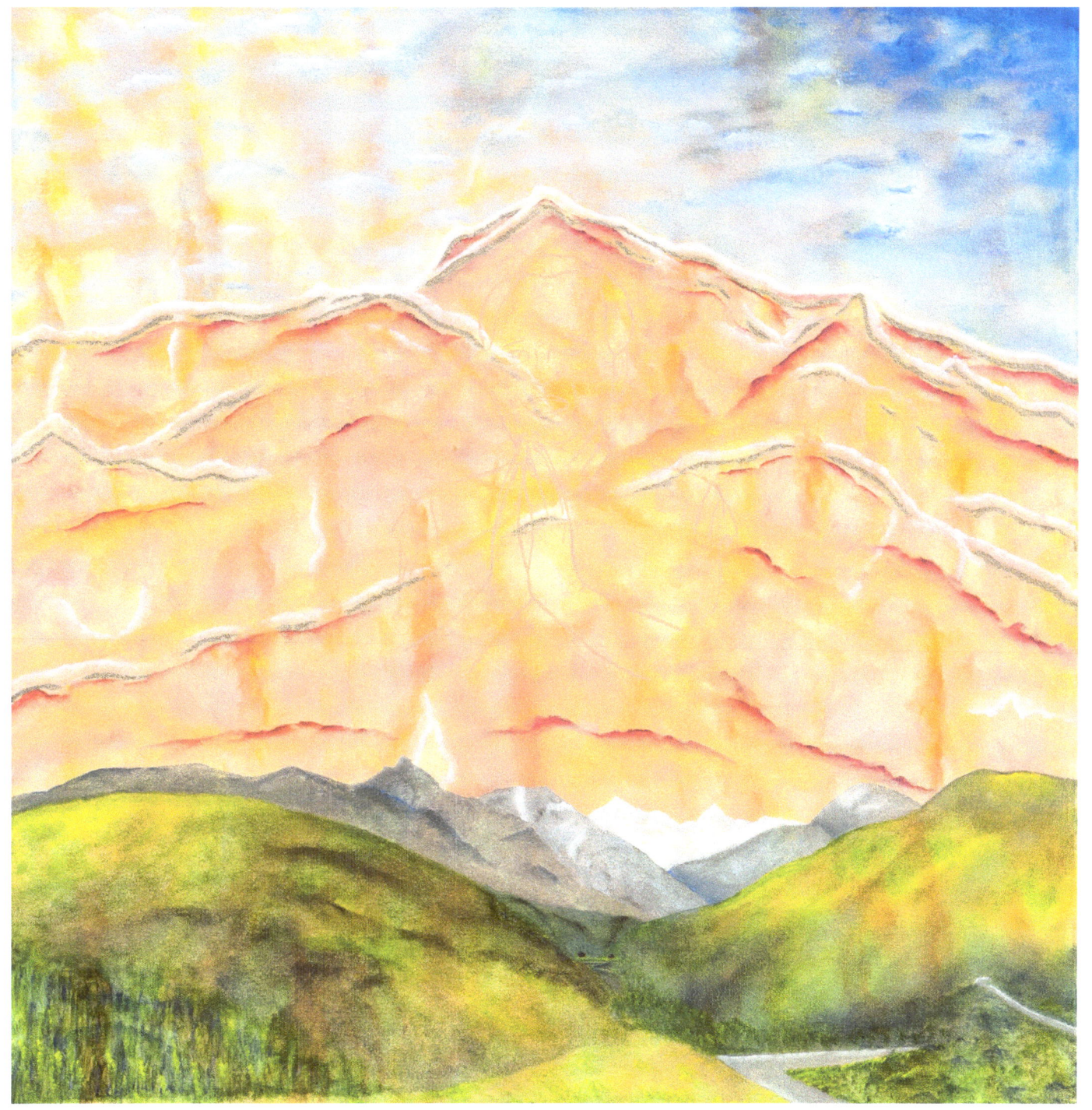

Form

www.ingramcontent.com/pod-product-compliance
Lightning Source LLC
Chambersburg PA
CBHW051046180526
45172CB00002B/541